Ginseng Growers' Guide

BY

J. I. MALONE

PUBLISHED IN THE ENGLISH LANGUAGE
BY
J. I. MALONE
CEDARBURG, WISCONSIN
1930

COPYRIGHT BY
J. I. MALONE
1930

J. I. MALONE
AUTHOR—GROWER

Dedicated to the cause of a healthier and happier American public, and for the propagation and growth of this Medical plant which is now being used by over 600,000,000 Chinese people.

CONTENTS

	PAGE
INTRODUCTION	ix
AMERICAN GINSENG	1
CHINESE GINSENG FIRM REPORT	5
The Future of Ginseng in China	5
The Present Ginseng Market in China	6
Reasons for our Ginseng Business Increase	7
THE GINSENG PLANT	13
Its Uses as a Medicine	15
The Ginseng Market	17
Statistics Showing Exports	18
Domestic Prices Exports	20
GROWING THE PLANT	23
Kind of Soil	24
Preparation of Soil	25
Fertilizer	26
Construction of Beds	28
Planting	29
Shading	32
The Growing Season	36
The Ginseng Seed	38
When to Dig Matured Roots	40
Drying Roots for Market	43
Its Cost and Profit	44

GINSENG DISEASES AND THEIR CONTROL . . 49
   Alternaria Blight 50
   Root-Rot and Phytophthora Mildew . . 51
   Thielavia Root-Rot 52
   Sclerotinia White and Black Rot . . . 52
   Damping Off of Seedlings 54
   Rust 55
   Spraying 55
DRAINAGE 59
   Cultivating and Mulching 59
   Protection of the Crop 61
SUMMARY 62

INTRODUCTION

TO ANSWER by personal letter all the inquiries and questions that come to this writer through the mail is impracticable, not to say impossible, and is what prompted the writing of this book. This literature is to cover the cultivation and marketing of this fascinating and very profitable plant, called Ginseng. At the same time all those questions should be answered, mainly for the preventing of misadventures and failures in Ginseng growing, and of keeping the cultivation of this profitable plant out of the hands of reckless exploiters.

The nature of this literature on Ginseng culture also deals with various diseases that sometimes attack this plant.

In the growing of Ginseng, the writer has given special attention, and has attempted to make his statements understandable to the beginner. In fact, throughout, he has tried to hold the needs of the beginner constantly in mind.

The writer became interested in Ginseng several years ago, and has been almost constantly engaged in the study and growing of it ever since, analyzing and experimenting in all the different phases of the plant, and an effort has been made to give the reader the benefit, in every event, of his own experiences and observations of his scientific studies.

The writer is largely indebted to many scientific writers and authorities, and a cheerful and grateful acknowledgment of these authorities has been made wherever they are quoted.

     Sincerely,
      J. I. MALONE,
   Cedarburg, Wisconsin.

AMERICAN GINSENG

GINSENG is a native product of recognized importance. The exporting of dry roots has existed for more than a century, and for the past 10 years has attained an average yearly export value of more than $2,000,000.

Ginseng is unknown to a large majority of people, and to raise it successfully it is necessary that the grower knows something of its nature and requirements. As a background, the reader should know something of its history.

The American Ginseng (panax quinquefolium) belongs to a family of plants closely related to the parsley family, in which are included the parsnip, celery and carrot. Our plant is a near relative of the Ginseng of China and Korea, and is highly prized by the Chinese. Europe, early in the eighteenth century, heard of its high value to the Chinese, and inquiries were made as to whether or not it grew in North America. A French Jesuit priest discovered that the Indians were using Ginseng in 1679 for medical purposes. These Jesuits were great missionary priests of the Roman Catholic Church, and went to the uttermost parts of the earth to spread the Christian gospel.

The French priest, having been to China, learned something of this Ginseng plant and the high value it had. Chinese had been raising this plant for hundreds of years and using it as a cure-all medicine, the same as they do today, but they could not grow nearly enough for their vast population, which is about five times greater than that of the United States. Their product was also of an inferior grade. Soon afterward the French began buying it through the agencies of the Indians and exporting it to China. The first discovery was near Montreal, Canada, and by the year 1750 was becoming a valuable export, and was found to be growing throughout the New England states. As the population moved Westward, it was found to be growing as far West as Wisconsin, Minnesota, Iowa, and South almost to the Gulf of Mexico. Wisconsin export alone is reported to have reached $80,000 in 1859, large quantities also being shipped from other states. As the years rolled by and immigrants came West, and settled down, the forests were cut down and consequently wild Ginseng became more and more extinct. In the wooded areas that were left the plant was very much sought after until soon the wild supply became almost exhausted. Small patches can still be found in certain areas but like wild fur-bearing animals, it will soon be a thing of the past; that is why we are raising it under natural conditions to supply the great demand.

A letter from a Chinese Ginseng firm with valuable information that one might want to know, dated September 16, 1929, makes up the next chapter in this book.

CHINESE GINSENG FIRM REPORT

"The Future of Ginseng in China"

FREQUENT requests from growers and shippers for information about the future of Ginseng in China have come to our office. It is our sincere belief that the medical value and general usefulness of Ginseng will never be lost in China. Through years of experience, the Chinese people have found Ginseng to possess medicinal properties of lasting value. Its market, therefore, in China will improve rather than decline with improved methods of communication, provided, of course, that the American growers will raise the highest grade of Ginseng roots.

"The Present Ginseng Market in China"

"WILD GINSENG: The wild Ginseng price inflation at the beginning of the present season was due to speculation on the part of some New York dealers. Their prices, compared with those in China, were far too high, which brought about the present drop, resulting in great losses to many shippers. Fortunately those who acted upon our information and advice did not suffer such losses. This shows how very valuable our service is to any and all shippers, and how necessary it is for them to establish connections with us.

"CULTIVATED GINSENG: According to our latest information from China, there is a special demand for Cultivated Ginseng, particularly the highest grade, of small and large sizes, attractive in shape and of golden color, well wrinkled and breaks snow-white, etc. If you have this kind of root, we shall pay you wild root prices. There is also a demand for the average grade variety. Whenever your crop is well dried and ready for market, send us a few pounds sample, and also notify us how many pounds your sample represents for our best valuation. If your lot is large enough we shall send our buyer specially to see you.

"Reasons for our Ginseng Business Increase"

"1. We are in a position to make the most attractive offers.
2. We do business with a large class of the best shippers in the United States and Canada.
3. We look after the interests of our shippers by supplying timely information on market conditions.

"Regardless of price fluctuations, we are always in the market for both Wild and Cultivated Roots in large or small quantities. It would pay you to become our shipper to insure a continuous flow of transactions. You will, therefore, get more money from us than from other dealers. WHY NOT GIVE US A TRIAL RIGHT NOW?"

"Present Prices"

WILD GINSENG	Per lb.
N. Y., N. Eng., N. Penn., Mich. & Canada	$17.50 to $16.00
N. J., N. Ohio, Ill., Ind., & Cent. Penn.	15.75 to 14.75
Minnesota, Wisconsin, Iowa, & S. Penn.	15.75 to 14.75
N. W. Vir., Cent. Ohio, Ill., Ind., & Md.	14.50 to 14.00
N. Carolina, & S. Ohio, Ill., & Indiana	14.00 to 13.50
W. Virginia, Missouri, & Tennessee	13.50 to 13.00
Kentucky & other Southern States	13.00 to 12.25

CULTIVATED GINSENG	Per lb.
Best Grades, Wild Transplanted (no fibre)	$13.50 to $10.00
Good Grades, Transpl. & Selected (no fibre)	10.00 to 8.00
Average Original Grades (no fibre)	7.50 to 5.00
Prongs	3.25 to 2.75
Fibre	2.25 to 1.85
Culls	3.00 to 2.00

"We shall guarantee the above prices until our next circular report. We suggest that you ship us your Ginseng promptly to take advantage of these prices before we issue our next quotations.

GINSENG FIRM REPORT

"We make cash payments on your shipments. Whenever you send us shipments, we shall hold the same separate for your approval on our quotations, and shall remit immediately when such quotations are accepted.

"Also we accept C.O.D. shipments with privilege of examination, and pay express and Parcel Post charges for lots of five pounds and over.

"Please fill out and return the enclosed postal card to us promptly that we may know when you will dig your crop and expect your shipment.

"We assure you that you will realize larger profits from our offers than from those of others. It is highly advisable, however, for you to consult us as to the market before you sell."

"SHIP YOUR GINSENG TO THE
CHINESE GINSENG FIRM."
WING COMPANY
Telephone Cortlandt 5813
5 Beekman Street   New York City, N. Y.

Under the present conditions of production, Ginseng offers attractive possibilities to patient cultivators who appreciate the limitations of growth, and the slow development of woodland plants in general, and are willing to make a material outlay with only scanty returns in view, for several years to come, but it holds no inducement for inexperienced growers looking for quick profits from a small investment. The culture of Ginseng is best begun in an inexpensive manner, enlarging the equipment only as reasonable success seems assured. For the conscientious man it holds wonderful possibilities and when once he becomes interested, will learn more and more from year to year, and by using common horse sense and a little guiding, will be on the road to success in an uncrowded line of work.

The Ginseng grower has an open market for his product. I've known of instances where several large buyers came to one Ginseng grower when his crop was ready to sell, and each buyer put in his bid on the crop. I know of a dozen large buyers and numerous smaller buyers and exporters who advertise almost constantly for Ginseng.

Almost every farmer raises wheat, barley, oats, or corn, and the vast production has lowered the price of these commodities. Something that's easy to do, everyone does. How many of you readers have heard of or seen a Ginseng farm? Not many, I believe. Well, here's an idea for you right now—raise something that everyone else is not raising. Ginseng is a proven product with regard to its medicinal qualities, and don't be a bit surprised if it will be used all over this country within the next few years. It has been used all over China and Japan for hundreds of years for all kinds of ailments, and it has been used as a medicine by the Indians in this country before the white man inhabited it. If you have any doubt as to its medical qualities, write me and I will see that you get a bottle of it put up in liquid form, manufactured by a Milwaukee concern, at the Factory price—a cure-all for almost any ailment mentionable. It is being introduced and sold from platforms with money-back guarantees, as "God's greatest gift to man," for the purpose of restoring health.

THE GINSENG PLANT

THE Ginseng plant is an erect perennial with a stem one foot long, and branches into three stalks at the top of the stem, and each stem is from 2½ to 3½ inches long, and at the end of each stem is a thin stalk which bears in July a greenish-white flower followed by berries, which develop rapidly until in August, turning red, inside of which are the seeds.

The part of the plant used commercially is the root, which is composed of two parts, the rootstalk at the top of the root and the root proper. The age of the root can be told by the number of scars caused by the stem from year to year. A bud, for the next year's growth, forms in August, and when digging for transplanting, this should not be disturbed or broken. In this locality, of Eastern Wisconsin, the plant comes through the ground in the early part of May and in about six weeks the leaves have attained their full size.

The natural home of the plant in its wild state has been from Maine all down through the Eastern states, including the Western part of South Carolina, and from Minnesota East and South to Northern Alabama. Years ago it grew in great abundance in all those states, but it was so energetically hunted, and the forest area so diminished, that it is now almost extinct. The plant has been grown domestically in many other states, especially in some of the Western states, including California and states North of it. The plant thrives remarkably well under cultivation on the rich prairie soil of the Middle West.

THE GINSENG PLANT

Its Uses as a Medicine

The root has always been used to some extent in this country, but chiefly in China. It is bought by dealers in this country as an article of export. The Chinese and Koreans value it very highly and indeed regard it as a remedy for nearly all diseases. It is used by all the rank and file of people, from the humblest citizen to high officials and emperors, and they have unlimited faith in its power to prevent and cure many of the ills of the human body. It has been noted that the short, chunky, plain shaped roots would bring a little better price, much the same as our products when brought to market, as a well shaped smooth potato will bring a better price than one that is ill-shaped and not smooth. The Chinese have their own ideas about right living and I dare say that it is better than ours. They know how to keep that human system well, and how to cure it when it is ill.

Personally I have had the opportunity to listen to lectures sponsored by a Milwaukee manufacturer placing this product on the market, and they have sold thousands of bottles of this Ginseng remedy since they started selling about four months ago. While mingling among the crowd at the lectures I have heard the highest of praise given to this medicine, and they always come back for more, besides telling their friends about its wonderful qualities. I have known it to cure people with chronic constipation, inflammatory rheumatism, kidney trouble, general run down condition, and many other ailments of the human body. This Ginseng root, combined with roots, herbs, barks and flowers of nature, acts directly on the inner organs of the body and puts them in a healthy, active condition to do the work they are supposed to do. There is no praise too great for the curative powers of Ginseng, and if its popularity spreads in other cities as it has in Milwaukee, it would not be long before the entire country would be awakened to its wonderful medicinal qualifications.

The Ginseng Market

In regard to the markets of Ginseng in the United States, it is bought up by dealers in nearly all large cities and by a great many fur buyers. Those buyers in smaller places resell it to large exporters, and they in turn export it to the Chinese markets. Several Chinese Ginseng firms are in direct contact with Chinese markets.

The prices paid recently by dealers in the business were $5.00 to $7.50 for the average grades, $8.00 to $10.00 for good grades, and $10.00 to $13.00 for the best grades per pound. Wild Ginseng brings about $4.00 to $5.00 per pound more than the Cultivated, but owing to the scarcity of the wild plant, very little is being shipped.

Statistics Showing Exports

This report is taken from the United States Bureau of Statistics of the Department of Agriculture and includes and covers the years 1860 to 1926.

Periods of Years	Pounds	Val. Av.	Val. per lb.
1860 to 1869	4,449,445	$ 3,902,209	$ 0.94
1870 to 1879	4,041,727	4,537,008	1.12
1880 to 1889	3,457,294	6,771,830	1.95
1890 to 1899	2,163,302	7,843,888	3.62
1900 to 1909	1,513,558	9,610,614	6.34
1910 to 1919	2,047,800	14,823,781	7.24
1920 to 1926	1,178,620	14,671,311	12.45

The prices of Cultivated Ginseng remain relatively high, and a continuance of the demand for American Ginseng may reasonably be expected.

The fact that American Ginseng is much sought after in China is emphasized by the following Government Report:

Mr. Quag, as head of the Chinese Merchants Company of Shanghai, China, which is a very large trading company in that country, says—

"The supply is fast diminishing: the demand is growing greater each year; and the amount used is only gauged by the supply. We pay a good price for your Ginseng; we would pay more if an increased price would get it. We could use twenty times what we get at present prices. It would be impossible for you Americans to glut the market with Ginseng in the next fifty years. Ginseng is used by every Chinaman, no matter how poor. The Ginseng market is as staple as the market for Tea or Coffee, and not subject to change as is every other article of commerce. Unless the Americans cultivate it there is going to be a great scarcity of Ginseng, and that soon."

The following are the Statistics of the Bureau of the Department of Agriculture:

Domestic prices, exports, and value of

20 GINSENG GROWERS' GUIDE

American Ginseng from 1900 to 1926, inclusive:

Domestic Prices (per pound) Exports

Year	Wild Root High	Wild Root Low	Cultivated Root High	Cultivated Root Low	Pounds	Total	Average value per pound
1900	$ 6.10	$ 2.75	$ 7.00	$4.00	160,901	$ 833,710	$ 5.18
1901	8.75	3.75	10.00	5.75	149,069	801,672	5.38
1902	6.35	3.00	8.00	3.00	154,063	856,515	5.55
1903	7.50	4.00	7.50	5.25	151,985	796,008	5.23
1904	8.10	5.00	8.00	7.00	131,882	851,820	6.45
1905	7.50	6.00	....	....	146,576	1,069,849	7.29
1906	7.50	6.00	7.00	4.00	160,949	1,175,844	7.30
1907	7.00	5.00	6.25	3.00	117,696	813,023	6.90
1908	7.00	4.50	6.25	4.00	154,180	1,111,994	7.21
1909	8.00	5.50	7.25	5.00	186,257	1,270,179	6.82
1910	8.00	5.50	7.25	5.00	192,406	1,439,434	7.48
1911	7.50	5.00	7.00	5.00	153,999	1,088,202	7.06
1912	9.00	5.00	7.50	3.00	155,308	1,119,301	7.20
1913	10.00	6.00	6.50	3.00	221,901	1,665,731	7.50
1914	11.50	6.00	8.00	3.00	224,605	1,832,686	8.15
1915	9.50	4.50	7.00	2.00	103,184	919,931	8.91
1916	11.00	5.00	6.50	3.00	256,082	1,597,508	6.23
1917	14.00	6.00	7.00	2.50	198,480	1,386,203	6.98
1918	19.00	9.50	9.00	3.00	259,892	1,717,548	6.60
1919	23.00	13.00	12.50	3.00	282,043	2,057,260	7.29
1920	23.00	10.00	12.00	3.00	160,050	1,875,348	11.71
1921	12.00	6.50	8.00	1.00	181,758	1,507,077	8.29
1922	16.00	7.00	12.00	2.00	202,722	2,334,993	11.51
1923	18.00	12.00	15.00	3.00	148,385	2,245,258	15.13
1924	16.50	11.00	14.00	2.00	167,318	2,399,926	14.35
1925	15.00	7.50	13.00	2.00	138,131	1,668,221	12.07
1926	19.00	10.00	13.00	3.00	180,262	2,640,488	14.65

Prices for 1900 to 1906 were obtained from dealers in Cincinnati, Ohio; Prices for 1907 to 1926 were compiled from Hunter-Trader-Trapper.

Exports are from Annual Reports of Foreign Commerce and Navigation of the United States.

Exports of 1926 are from Monthly Summary of Foreign Commerce of the United States, December, 1926.

22 GINSENG GROWERS' GUIDE

Bed 4 feet wide

Path 18 inches wide

Bed 4 feet wide

Path 18 inches wide

Bed 4 feet wide

Path 18 inches wide

Bed 4 feet wide

Path 18 inches wide

Laying out a field in beds for Ginseng (Top view)

GROWING THE PLANT

OVER twenty-five years ago some of the first attempts were made at growing Ginseng under cultivation. Shortly after 1900 rumors went around far and wide that if one wanted to become wealthy very quickly, all he had to do was to invest a small amount in Ginseng and his dream was realized, and to invest a few hundred dollars would make him a millionaire in a few years' time. This rumor no doubt was spread by some "get rich quick artist" and not a grower of Ginseng. This so-called boom lasted but a short time and cost some investors considerable money. The cause of this early failure in the business was caused mainly by improper means and ways of growing the plant under cultivation, and ignorance of the means of drying it for the market. Years of experimenting have proven that the plant can be grown very successfully under cultivation. We are learning new ways of doing things all the time. As the old saying goes, "We are never too old to learn," and this holds true of Ginseng.

Kind of Soil

To transfer a wild plant from its natural home to an artificial one, conditions must be somewhat the same, shading, slope of soil, etc. Soil and location are very important. Ginseng naturally grows on slopes of ravines on well-drained soil. The soil should be fairly light and dry, on the order of good garden soil that is capable of raising good vegetables. New soil with good drainage is the best that can be had. Ginseng plants have been found to grow the best in localities where hardwood timber has once grown. Sandy

GROWING THE PLANT

soil should be avoided. In many cases the addition of leaf mold from hard woods has given best results, since Ginseng requires an acid soil, a deep, rich, loamy soil, free from hard pan subsoil, which absorbs excessive water during wet weather, and not have pools of water remaining on the surface. Ginseng will not grow well with "wet feet." Two inches of rich humus, which is black earth with decomposed leaves, and other vegetable matter, is the real food for the plant.

Preparation of Soil

The preparation of the soil should be begun in the middle of Summer, to give time for working the soil over several times before planting. If a small patch is to be used, a spading fork can be used, but if a larger piece of ground is being prepared, a team with a plow and disk-harrow, and spring tooth-harrow, will do the job very nicely. Plow about eight or nine inches deep, Here is where we can improve on the natural home of the plant, by making the soil loose and mellow. When well worked up this soil will have a depth of about twelve inches. Never work up clay soil in wet weather, because when it dries, it will have a tendency to cake. Sod soil should be plowed in early Summer to give it a chance to decay, and it will mix well with the sub-soil.

Fertilizer

After the ground has been well worked up several times, it is time for the fertilizers. Overfeeding of fertilizer is not recommended. If barnyard manure is to be used, it should be well rotted. Raw bone meal has been used with good results, to the extent of three or four quarts to a square rod, twice a year. Chemical fertilizers of different kinds have been used, but with injurious results. Some of the best results have been obtained from hard-

GROWING THE PLANT

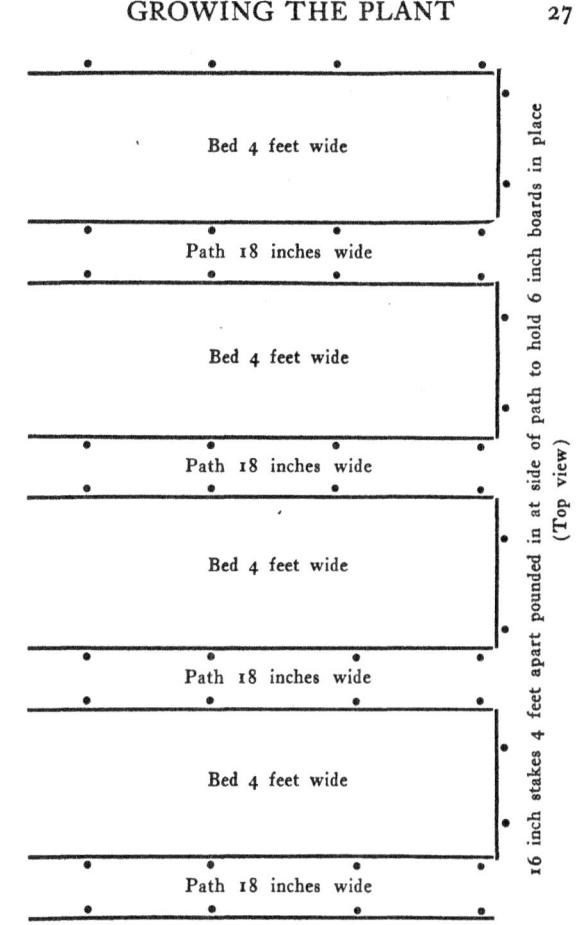

Bed 4 feet wide

Path 18 inches wide

Bed 4 feet wide

Path 18 inches wide

Bed 4 feet wide

Path 18 inches wide

Bed 4 feet wide

Path 18 inches wide

16 inch stakes 4 feet apart pounded in at side of path to hold 6 inch boards in place
(Top view)

wood leaf-mold and old rotted hardwood sawdust.

Construction of Beds

For various reasons it is best to lay the garden out in beds. For economy of space and convenience, make the beds four feet wide, with a path eighteen inches between. The length of the beds is immaterial. Four feet is a convenient width for planting and weeding. Beds are not to be stepped on at any time.

The ground is taken from the paths and thrown into ridges. A string is drawn along the side of the path and stakes sixteen inches long are driven into the ground, about four feet apart, and boards six inches wide are placed along outside the path. In heavy soils the beds can be slightly elevated for draining off surface water. The beds are then leveled off, slightly rounded on the surface, and we are then ready for planting.

Planting

Planting can be done in the Spring or Fall, but Fall planting is recommended in preference to Spring. Planting is usually done from the middle of September until almost freezing up time. The shipping of plants or seed in warm express cars in early Spring have the danger of sprouting in shipment. Spring planting has the disadvantage of a late wet Spring, and the ground cannot be gotten into proper shape. If seeds are planted they can be put into a nursery bed, $1\frac{1}{2}$ x $1\frac{1}{2}$ inches apart. Fifty per cent germination has been considered a fair stand, although in some cases reaching seventy-five per cent. Seeds are to be planted to a depth of 1 or $1\frac{1}{2}$ inches with loose earth, or leaf mold. When seeds are exposed to the sun or dry wind for a short time, they soon die, and will not germinate.

Ginseng roots are to be planted six to

eight inches apart each way. A garden hoe is used and a "V" shaped trench is made across the bed and the plants are laid in this trench the desired distance apart, so that the bud of the plant is covered about one inch in depth, another trench is dug and the dirt is used to cover the row just planted.

Another very good, and easier method, is to lay the roots on top of the finished bed and through ground from the next bed on top of the plants to a depth of one or one and one-half inches. Start at one end or side of the garden and when one bed is planted level off the next bed, etc. Never allow the plants to lay without covering them.

Leaves or straw are then used to cover the beds after planting, and is used as a mulch and protects the plants from drying out, and keeps the ground mellow; prevents the growth of many kinds of weeds, and, as it decays, adds to the fertil-

8 foot posts set in ground 11 feet apart each way
(Top view)

ity of the soil. In the Fall cover the leaves or straw with two inch mesh poultry netting to keep it in place. This covering of three or four inches helps to prevent the plants from alternate freezing and thawing, which is sometimes injurious, although freezing does not harm the plant in any way. In regard to freezing, Ginseng is a very hardy plant, the ground often being frozen very deep in this Northern climate.

Roots before planting must always be kept in a damp atmosphere and never allowed to dry out, and the plant must never be bent or cramped in planting it.

Shading

Ginseng, being a native of the forest, requires shade, not a dense shade, because some sunlight is very necessary to its growth. In this Northern climate, about eighty per cent of the sunlight must be shut out, allowing about twenty per cent of sunlight to penetrate through the shading. In Southern states, the shading should be a little denser. A cheaply constructed shading for a small patch can be made by placing posts a short distance apart and use cross-poles from one to the other, and cover with brush and branches. But here is a more practical way: place eight foot posts one and one-half feet in the ground to the side of the paths, eleven feet apart each way, extending six and one-half feet above the ground. Now use 12 foot 2 x 4's from top of one post to the top of the other, and bolt them together, using 20 penny spikes between them, nailed in the top of the post to hold them in place. Now for the shading itself.

Use plaster lath, four feet long, nailed on separate sections, which consist of boards 1 inch by 3 inches by 12 feet long. Put laths about one-third inch apart, and 1 foot from one end of boards. Use three boards for each section, one on each side and one in the center. Cut boards on a slant one foot from one end, so it will fit under the next section when placed up on the 2 by 4's. A form is used for making the sections by which the boards are put in, and nails with the heads filed off are nailed into the form for the purpose of spacing the laths. Use 68 laths for a section eleven feet long.

This form for making sections works wonderfully well, and when placed in a warm shed or stable it can be used during the cold Winter months for making shading, to be used in the Spring, when the plants come through the ground. Heavy snow-falls during the Winter months sometimes break the sections, so it is advisable to pile four in a row up on top of the 2 by 4's, this fourth one being wired down, to prevent any high wind from blowing the sections off during the Summer. The sides of the garden should be fenced so as to keep out dogs, cats, rabbits,

GROWING THE PLANT

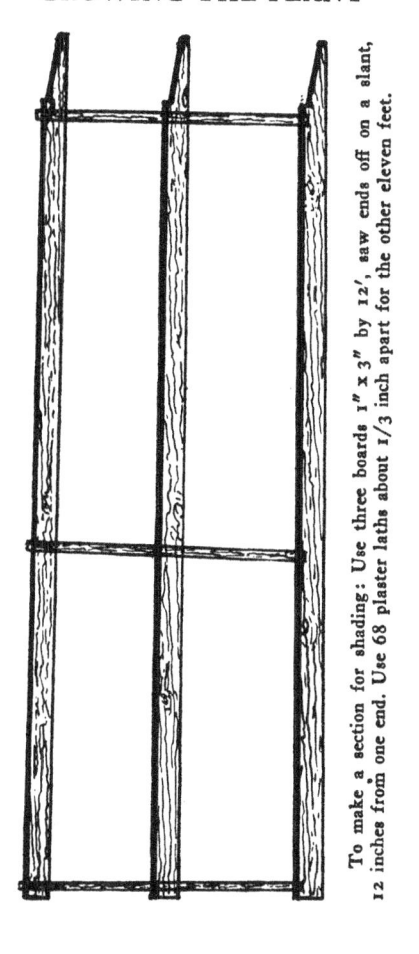

To make a section for shading: Use three boards 1" x 3" by 12', saw ends off on a slant, 12 inches from one end. Use 68 plaster laths about 1/3 inch apart for the other eleven feet.

or any other larger animals. Chickens can be kept out by the use of poultry netting. On the South and West sides, shading is needed, but the East and North sides do not.

Ginseng can also be grown under the natural shade of a woods, but when this is done, all the small trees and roots must be removed. If all the small roots of trees are allowed to grow, they will often sap the nourishment and moisture needed by the plant, although the plant has been grown very successfully in partly shaded woods.

The Growing Season

There is comparatively little work to do with the beds during the Summer season. Weeds do not grow well in shade, and those that do grow can be pulled out. One man can take good care of a three acre patch alone. Ginseng will stand as much dry weather as any garden vegetable and therefore does not need any

GROWING THE PLANT 37

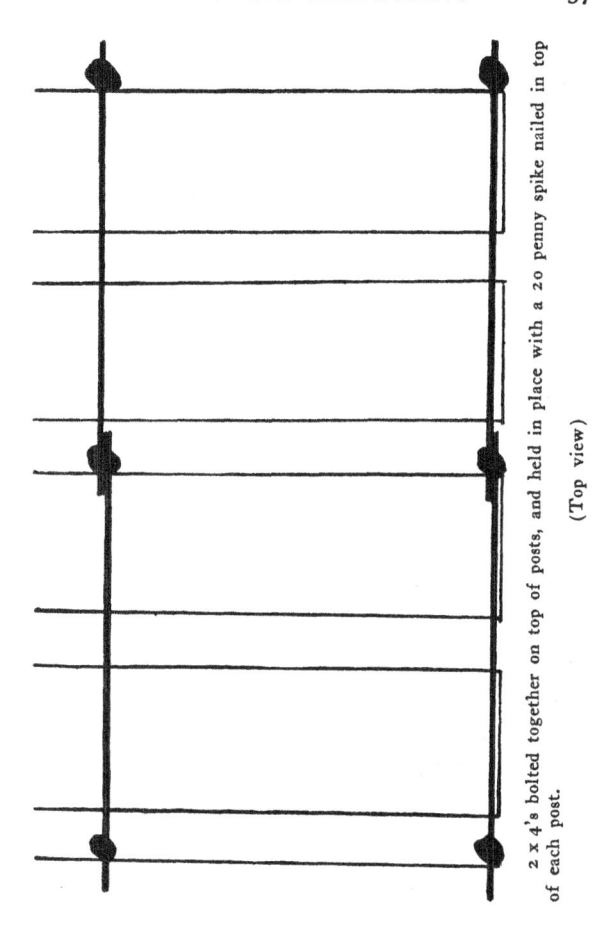

2 x 4's bolted together on top of posts, and held in place with a 20 penny spike nailed in top of each post.

(Top view)

watering unless in cases of continued dry, hot weather.

In the Spring when the frost is out of the ground, it is advisable to see that the leaves or straw are not matted together, preventing the young plants from coming through. After the poultry netting has been taken off, use a four or five tined fork, and go up and down each side of the beds loosening all the covering; sometimes it mats closely on the ground preventing the plants coming through.

The Ginseng Seed

The two profitable crops of Ginseng is the seed and roots. Seed begins to ripen the first part of September and continues until the latter part of the month. Some of the seed ripen earlier than the rest and should be picked off accordingly, or they will drop. When the clusters of seed turn red they are ripe.

Unlike most other seed it loses its vital-

Ginseng beds in middle of Winter with a good blanket of snow, also the supports waiting for Spring and the shading, on the J. I. Malone farm, Cedarburg, Wis.

Top and side sections ready to be placed upon the supports in Spring.

ity when allowed to become dry. When allowed to remain dry for a short time, the seed dies. Ginseng will not germinate until eighteen months after it is harvested, and during all this time it must be kept moist and damp. It must retain a happy medium, not too dry, or not too wet, or it will rot. The seed could be planted right after harvesting it, but here again lies the danger of the ground becoming too dry or too wet.

A better system is used and this is by means of stratifying the seed. It is done with a box and damp sand. Bore holes in the bottom of the box and cover the holes with a fine screen to allow any excess water to escape. Then put two inches of damp sand in the bottom of the box, and put a layer of seed on top of the sand, close together, but not on top of each other. Another layer of one inch of sand on top of seed, etc. Place the box in a cool cellar.

After the seed has been in the box a year, sift it out and plant it in nursery beds, broadcast, or about an inch apart. Care must be taken never to allow the seed to dry out in any way.

Some growers transplant the roots when they are one year old, but it is more advisable to transplant them at the end of the second year.

When plants are two years old, some of them will bear a few seed. In the third year an average of twelve to fourteen; in the fourth year about twenty-five to thirty seeds; and in the fifth year an average of thirty-five to forty.

When to Dig Matured Roots

The time to dig matured roots for market is in Fall, after the tops begin to die down, and when they have completed their fifth season's growth. In some cases growers have dug the roots when they were four years old, which is perfectly

Top view showing the sections piled in rows, to insure against breakage by heavy snow, on the J. I. Malone farm, Cedarburg, Wis.

Side view of the same gardens. The foot and a half of snow is undisturbed by strong winds.

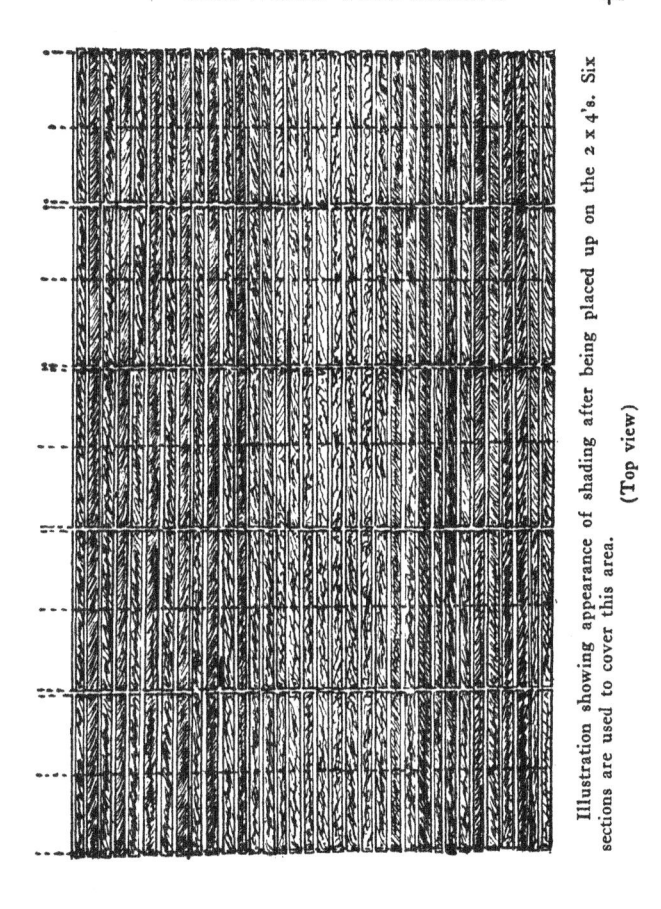

Illustration showing appearance of shading after being placed up on the 2 x 4's. Six sections are used to cover this area. (Top view)

all right, but it pays to leave them another year or two.

Before beginning to dig, remove all the leaves and straw, and then pull all the stems or tops off. With a spading fork or manure fork, start at one end of the bed and dig almost full depth of the teeth of the fork. A digging machine has not been perfected yet to do the work.

The roots are then sorted out and all small roots transplanted, instead of being sold, sometimes many seedling plants are found which were grown from seed fallen off the plant from year to year.

A good way to wash roots after digging is to use a wash tub half filled with roots, and covered with water, and then stirred around with a broom. Change the water several times, and the roots are found to be a nice, clear white color. But do not use a scrubbing brush, as it will scratch and break the outer skin.

Upper picture showing Ginseng garden in the fall.
Lower picture showing the making of new beds for the transplanting of roots.

Drying Roots for Market

After roots are well cleaned, they should be spread out in a warm, airy room. Some growers spread them outside in the Autumn sun to dry, but the weather does not always remain the same, some days being rainy and damp, and this, therefore, is not a very reliable way.

After the first week in this warm, airy room, the temperature can be raised 85 to 90 degrees, and a little circulation of air allowed to pass through. All the fine roots and fibres are now to be broken off, and roots again spread out to dry. Wire shelves made of fine poultry netting are very desirable.

In about three weeks' time, or probably a little longer, when the roots become dry, they are ready to be shipped in bags or boxes to the market.

Growers are advised against sending green roots to market, and when shipped before they are dry, the dealer will pay accordingly, allowing for shrinkage in weight. In drying, the roots will shrink to about one-third of their weight when green.

Its Cost and Profit

Now that's the big question that has been asked this grower, through the mail and otherwise, and is much more easily asked than answered. I would say very frankly that it would require a whole lot of extra bookkeeping to answer the question correctly. There are one year, two years, three years, four years, and five years, so you see that you are taking care of five different crops at the same time.

However, no one should rush into the growing of this crop on a large scale who has not familiarized himself with the subject. Common sense will tell that. There are perils and profits in this line of work, as there are in any other business. This is for conscientious workers—with a certain amount of patience, and with proper care and attention large profits may be realized. Approach the problem cautiously and studiously. After reading this book, the reader will know whether or not he will join this fascinating line of work. To the investor who can wait until his crop materializes, large profits may be realized. Under favorable circumstances, one acre of ground is capable of producing about 4,000 pounds of dry roots at the end of the fifth year's growth, sold at a low average of $8.00 per pound or even a little less, brings in a very handsome return on the investment.

Profits, after all, interest most of us more than any other part of the proposition. Profits depend mostly on the growers' ability, and it is a poor policy to figure out for someone else his return on an investment. Where some are financially successful, others may fail, that is true in any line of business, and is also true of the Ginseng business.

Some of the very prosperous and successful Ginseng growers of today started growing it as a side line some years ago, and went into the business stronger and stronger. An article in the American Magazine some months ago interested me greatly concerning their start in Ginseng on a small patch of ground behind their house, much to their father's anger, who did not know what it was. They had the staying qualities of successful men, and today they are the largest growers in the world, having sold close to a half million dollars worth in the last few years. When I was employed in their Ginseng gardens several years ago, I became very interested in this fascinating little plant, and learned to go about growing it myself, in their most up-to-date method of growing and taking care of it. Two brothers, who had been class-mates of mine in High School, after graduation became financial partners of those first growers, and are now some of the most wealthy and influential men in this part of the state. Their growth from almost nothing, was remarkable, as well as interesting. Those same Ginseng growers are also interested in the silver fox business, and are now the world's largest raisers of foxes. They herald as the two most profitable businesses today the silver fox and the Ginseng business.

Being personally acquainted with these men it is interesting to note their small and meager start from almost nothing, to be today the biggest in their line of business—in other words, the captains of industry. It is the romance of any business that is interesting, no matter what it is, growing from a small beginning to one of the biggest.

The following experiment of financial

success may be interesting to any prospective Ginseng grower:

An investment of $1,850 over a period of 8 years. Average per cent of net profits, 135% per year. The entire capital invested was paid back at the end of the sixth year with 6% interest, and after that an average of 350% per year. The area of ground occupied was a little over one-third of an acre.

The way to grow the best roots is to not allow the plant to bear seed, the bud bearing the seed being nipped off in early Summer, with a scissors or pen knife. In China some of the growers practice this, although unknown to most growers in this country. The selection of seed plants should be made at digging time, and only from well shaped roots.

GINSENG DISEASES AND THEIR CONTROL

MANY of the troubles of plants in regard to disease have been traced to two causes, namely, insects and parasitic fungi or bacteria.

Most of this valuable information is contributed through experiments by the United States Department of Agriculture, regarding the symptoms, cause and control of the various diseases attacking the Ginseng plant. Taking the wild plant from its native forest and placing it under cultivation adapted it more readily to attacks from disease. The same is true of wild animals when placed in captivity, and raised in abundance for commercial reasons.

At first very little was known regarding the remedy and cure of those plant diseases, but great strides have been made in the last few years. Governmental experiment stations did a great deal in controlling diseases, and also individual growers experimented with the maladies that attacked their crop.

Alternaria Blight

Small spots first appear on the stem, the next year large dead spots appear on the leaves. The leaves when infected near the stem drop off very readily, and when it attacks the clusters of seed, they will shell, and in some cases, fall off. The disease is caused by a fungi, and not an insect.

Very satisfactory results have been obtained by the use of Bordeaux mixture 3-3-59. A new product that has been placed upon the market within the last few years called "Pyrox" is very good and used constantly by many successful growers. Spray the beds just before the plants come through the ground and continue to spray until they are up. The second application when leaves are fully expanded. Third application just after blossoming, in order to protect the seed heads.

The Alternaria disease is the most common and best known of Ginseng diseases, and the most easily controlled.

Root-Rot and Phytophthora Mildew

This disease affects the leaves, stems and roots of all ages, and is very destructive. In some sections it has been very destructive. The leaves begin to droop at the base, both leaves and stems becoming discolored, and spots resembling Alternaria blight appear. The disease is caused by a fungi and when the root begins to rot it causes a disagreeable odor, something like vegetable decay. The disease sometimes begins at the root, and continues upward, or begins at the top and moves downward.

The same remedy as used for Alternaria blight may be used. Too much wet, moist ground is the cause of most of these diseases, and the fact about good drainage can not be too strongly emphasized. Land that is well tile drained very seldom has very much trouble with this disease.

Thielavia Root-Rot

This disease is mostly found in seedling plants, and renders them worthless. It has a grayish-black appearance, never penetrating very deep into the root.

Acid phosphate applied to land at the rate of a ton to an acre has an action against this disease.

Sclerotinia White and Black-Rot

This is a vegetable disease attacking cucumbers, beets, lettuce, and is found in many Ginseng gardens.

It affects the stem and root, but not the foliage, and is a fungus, and is thread-like, up to a half inch in length. This disease is found especially where there is an abundant supply of moisture, here again stressing the fact about good drainage.

Formaldehyde, 1 part to 50 parts of water, or copper sulphate, 1 pound to 10 gallons of water, disinfected into the soil after the diseased plants are removed.

Black-rot originally was a forest disease affecting wild plants, and affected plants die and do not come up in the Spring. The surface of the plant becomes black and works into the root. The disease is a soil fungus and can be disinfected with a solution of Formaldehyde, 1 part to 50 parts of water.

Damping Off of Seedlings

Damping off of Seedlings is caused by excessive moisture and lack of ventilation. The stems of affected plants become soft and rot at the surface of the soil, and the tops drop over.

Drainage and ventilation are of the greatest importance in raising seedlings. Growers have tried sprinkling one-fourth inch of sand on top of soil, during growing season, with good results. Disinfection of the soil with a solution of Formaldehyde, 1 part to 50 parts of water, is generally accepted as controlling the disease.

A papery leaf-spot appears during dry seasons, but does not spread from plant to plant. The spots are of a yellowish tint from small and circular, to large and oblong. It appears between the veins in the leaves.

This trouble is caused by lack of rainfall, and consequently lack of moisture in the ground, insufficient shade causing rapid drying out of the moisture.

As indicated in the foregoing, the only remedy that can be suggested is the correction of unfavorable conditions. Tile drainage should be used to equalize the moisture, and protect the plants in dry seasons. When plants are placed near large trees having long roots, they will rob the soil of very much moisture.

Rust

Rust attacks only the roots, causing them to appear rusty, but never attacks the tops, and affected plants reach maturity.

No satisfactory way of controlling rust has been found, but good results have been obtained by sterilizing the soil with steam.

Spraying

Spraying is done to protect the plant from attacks of parasitic fungi or insects, very much the same as spraying is done on apple trees and other garden plants.

Bordeaux mixture, until the last few years, has been a very good reliable spray for Ginseng. Since that time new commodities have come on the market. Science and research has put several different spray materials on the market, among them being "Ginseng Special" and "Pyrox," both of which have proven to be very good. If properly used, either of those materials will hold in check the Alternaria blight, as well as Mildew, and a stimulating effect is noticeable on plants affected with other diseases not directly controlled by spraying.

Mix 9 pounds to 50 gallons of water and spray soil thoroughly in the Spring just before the plants appear. Second application when plants have just pushed through the ground. Third application, when leaves are fully expanded. Fourth application, just after blossoms fall to protect seed heads, and again when the berries are almost full grown. Later applications can be made every two weeks throughout the season.

The under side of the leaves may also be sprayed but this is not absolutely necessary. One spraying under the leaves will sometimes last for two months. Ginseng plants are like most any other plant, in regard to disease and insects. They all have to be sprayed to get the best results. A successful orchard man or potato grower will spray his crops several times a season.

The old saying "An ounce of prevention is worth a pound of cure," holds just as true of your Ginseng garden as it does to anything else.

If hand power is to be used, it takes two men to do the job. High pressure, and a fine spray nozzle, is to be used. A ¼ or ⅜ inch hose, 75 feet long, used between the paths, works out very conveniently. A milk can with a spray pump in it can be used. A spray pump with an agitator at the bottom must be used, and never use one that does not keep the spray material mixed at all times. Never use an inclosed pressure tank that does not require pumping all the time. Some growers use small tanks that they pump up and carry on their backs, and spray until the pressure runs down.

A sprayer like that does not keep the materials properly mixed and the first part of the solution, when forced through the nozzle, is very thin, while the latter part has become very thick, because the spray material in the water has a tendency to settle to the bottom, consequently a very uneven distribution on the plants.

DRAINAGE

GINSENG beds should be laid out on a location with a gentle slope; some growers preferring the North or West slope, but this is not particularly necessary. To get the best results, drainage with four inch tile is suggested, in rows twelve to sixteen feet apart, to a depth of 2½ to 3½ feet deep, depending on the kind of soil, 2½ feet deep in clay soil and 3½ feet in sandy soil. Four inch cement tile are the standard size used, usually running crossways to the beds.

Cultivating and Mulching

There is very little cultivating to be done, but the weeds and grass have to be pulled out. If signs of caking on the surface occur, it should be scratched with the tines of a fork. One man can easily care for about three acres of Ginseng.

In all localities the beds are to be mulched with either straw or sawdust or leaves, held in place with two inch mesh poultry netting the width of the bed. Material containing weed seed should be avoided. When straw is used, a good suggestion is to run it through the grain separator a second time to separate the weed seed. Straw containing Canadian Thistle seed has caused an extra amount of work after the seed came up in the Ginseng beds. A mulch of about four inches is used in the Northern climate, while less can be used in the South. It is best to remove this mulch for awhile in the Spring, until all the small plants come through the ground. If a Winter mulch is not applied, the freezing and thawing in the Spring will damage the plants by heaving and lifting. In the Summer the mulch will hold in a great amount of moisture, keeping the ground cool, which is favorable to Ginseng plants.

During the Winter months moles often invade the Ginseng patch, and dig under and through the beds, eating some of the roots. Several kinds of mole traps are on the market, which work very well in this regard. Poisoned wheat placed near the bottom of the posts is very effective.

Protection of the Crop

Owing to the high value of the Ginseng crop, means must be taken to protect it against thieves, which is common with this high priced product. In former years the trouble seemed to be more common than it is now, many growers having suffered large losses. Burglar alarms have been installed around Ginseng patches and buildings in which the roots were stored for drying.

SUMMARY

THE writer has prepared this book to give the reader the benefit, in every case, of his own experience and observation and of his scientific studies and researches.

Being in constant touch with literature, furnished by Government Experiment Stations, he has gone a long way in solving many of the problems of this interesting and fascinating plant.

After reading the contents of this book and then getting prices of nursery stock from some reliable grower, the reader can easily figure out the cost of starting a Ginseng garden. As was said before, the problem should be approached cautiously and studiously. This is not a game for plungers, by any means. It is for the clear thinking, conscientious, ambitious, patient, hard-working man, who puts his heart and soul in the work. You doubtless have heard of plungers in other businesses—well, there are perils in every business. With proper care and attention, large profits can be realized. Proper care and attention, combined with intelligent effort and willingness, are the secrets of success in this business.

Sincerely,
J. I. MALONE,
Cedarburg, Wisconsin.

PRINTED IN
THE UNITED STATES OF AMERICA
BY
MOREHOUSE PUBLISHING CO.
MILWAUKEE, WIS.